Let There Be 9

Enneagram Poetry

Teshelle Combs

Teshelle Combs Books

Copyright © 2020 by Teshelle Combs

All Rights reserved, including the rights of reproduction in print or online in any whole or partial form.

Manufactured in the United States of America.

Book layout and design by Nate Combs Media.

ISBN-13: 979-8604609422

For the all of us.

Teshelle Combs

One

Perfect Pitch

The only thing that counts

Is what comes first.

There is no list,

No second best.

If perfect can be had,

We will all make it ours

If you would only

listen.

8

To Attain

Not to be best, but to be better

Not to be first, but to be faster

Not to be good, but to be greater

Not to be smart, but to be wiser

Order

There is a way.

Let us not pretend

Cacophony is

Destiny.

I've seen the webs, the lines, the current.

Trust me,

There is a way.

The Simplicity Of Corruption

I fear nothing.

It is a waste of time.

And time cannot be wasted.

I am confident

That I will either save the world

Or break it.

There is no fear in that.

Only what is and isn't.

Either logical villany

Or villainous logic.

Reformation

I seek not to be understood.

Care not if I'm undersold.

I want the undertaking.

Where the world can go,

It has not gone before.

I will only be worth it,

If all this is worth it.

And I am under no delusions.

I am worth it.

Two

Defining Existence

Love is the point

Though to call it such

Gives it no justice.

It is a fixed moment

That spreads like oceans

And fills the void of us.

I hold in my palm

In the smile of my eyes

In the words of my lips

In the swing of my arms

The whole point

Of it all.

14

Name

I am helping you.

No, no. It is not what I am *doing*.

It is who I am.

It is who I've been.

You can't see

The identity

In the bleed of my knees

Or the food you eat

Or the way I please?

I am

Helping You.

Sad. Also Tired.

In every step

There comes from me

A groan as deep

As a buried seed.

I say yes. I say yes. I say yes.

Please, stop asking.

I have nothing left.

Secret

I tremble.

I do.

Because

For all the

Loving you...

I will remain

For all my days

unloved.

I Don't Know How She Does It

I cannot work my magic

If I'm seen.

Nor can I let you

Get to know me.

Part of the plan

Is to empty me out

My life upends

Like the content of clouds.

If you were to see

The truest me

You would weep.

This, my love, my love,

Can never be.

So I will keep

invisible.

Three

Achieve

I show up.

I show up.

I show up.

I show up.

I show up.

I show up.

When can I stop?

I show up.

No Mistakes

I am breathtaking. I have always been.

Effortless. I unfold like flame.

Golden. First place. First place alone.

The medal I bear. The pressure. The weight.

The pressure. The weight. And no mistakes.

Always Never

I am always winning, but I never win

I am always running, but it's never the end

I am always striving, but it's never success

I am always first, but never the best

Worth

When you count what I've done

And who I've become

And it's time to say

My name

I may

Be

Hollow.

And you may not be

Proud

After all.

Watch This

I can do better.

I can be better.

Put me up!

Put me in!

I won't miss

I won't lose

I won't fail

I won't fall

If you

Promise me

You will see.

Four

Bi

Star grabber

Back stabber

Canopy soul

Midnight hole

Wild heart

Pointless art

Songs of praise

Cutting phase

Poetry

Pharisee

Perfect love

Final shove

Up and

Down we

go.

26

Don't you do it.

Don't you dare.

If ever you loved me

If ever you cared.

I have to be

I want to be

Please don't leave me

Alone.

The Paradox Of Me

Dig through the mud of me.

Make me a well.

Can you find what I left

In the wake of the storm?

Am I enough to capture your interest

In the prison of my chest,

Undercurrent and the shipwrecked soul.

In the murmur of my dreams?

I love you and it's lost

The moment I say it.

I need you and I'm lost

The moment you feel it.

Let me be real.

Please, God, let me be real.

28

Quake

I might wake up one day

And realize I am

Absolutely

No one.

After The Dark

You'll see.

They'll see.

One morning

When the sun comes up

I will rise too.

Good enough.

Glorious.

You'll see.

They'll see.

And maybe I'll see,

Too.

Five

I Don't Know

...

To Endure

Litany of obtrusion.

Constant steeping.

Prodding of misnomers.

Factual acrument.

Unprecedented uninvolvement.

Belittling regard.

Monastical reversion.

Insomniac epiphany.

When will you see

Or at least begin to believe

A mind can love?

Passive Voice

Watching is doing

When I do it

Next to you.

Nightmare

That there would be an imperative moment

And the love I have will not be functional

And the things I know will not be formidable

And it will be too late to change who I am

And also I can't.

Questionable Sources

Here is a truth that is almost constant

And dare I say near heretical

Pretty much perfect in its use

And something no one can disprove.

When it comes down to any number of things,

Or if it comes down to only one,

And no matter when the coming down comes

Or how many or if there's none

The answer is

It depends.

Six

Full Of Care

Careful, be careful.

Be careful with you.

Be careful, be careful

Be careful with me.

Be graceful and honest.

Be fragile and free.

As long as you're careful,

Then careful we'll be.

Discerment

I have a knack

For seeing through

To the very heart

Of every truth.

And all the fear

Of most of the fate

And the, "promise me you won't be late,"

Is because I've seen through

To the heart of you.

You have my protection

Whatever you choose.

Nobility

Maybe you won't see

Until the very end

Of the very end

Of all the days

I'll be given

That I will never be shaken

Or turned

Or lost

Or lured.

I said I would.

I said I would.

I will.

40

Lost

Upon looking up

To see that the footsteps

I have been following

Have vanished.

And to take one

Myself

In some direction

Unknown

With shifting sands

And dusk at hand.

Certain Uncertainty

I am leaking my own air

And squeezing my own brain

And swirling my own thoughts

And digging my own grave.

I just know it.

But I can take one breath.

I can ease my grasp.

I can settle it down.

I can rest.

Probably.

Seven

Any Of The Ways

Out loud

Let us be happy.

The world is just around the bend

At the top of the peak

Or in the late night rush.

We can run straight ahead

Or roll down the hill.

We can wake up at dawn.

So come

Let us be happy.

Proximal

I know, I know

The starting has just begun

But look. Look. Look!

See there?

Something is coming

Next.

Easy

There is a lightness to you

That calls out to me.

A new boat on the water

And the sun through the cracks.

Like the pluck of fresh strings

On a crisp diamondback.

Alone is the gray and the dull and the bleak.

With you there is brilliance and purpose and we.

46

Pain

Back against the wall

And…

Let us just skip this one.

And move on.

Weightless and restless

I see on the horizon

Everything.

Let's Go

Eight

The Push

I have in me

Both a compass

And a gun.

You are either coming

Or I am going.

I recommend

You come on.

Deal Breakers

To decide is to become

Worth the decision.

To hesitate it to ensure

Hesitation is yours in return.

To doubt is to be

Doubted.

Either close the deal

Or close the casket.

Fight Me

I cannot be the

Protector (of lost things)

If I become one of them.

52

Evolution

When I was

Not yet me

I couldn't do

What I can now

I had small fists

Small words

And a small place.

I will never return.

You cannot make me

Anymore.

Be My We

I crave the impossible.

The thrill of the hunt

Everyone feels when

They see the monsters.

The steady pulse

In my neck

When they don't

Scare me

At all.

We.

Will.

Win.

Nine

Relax

The still of a cool afternoon

And a ceiling fan on low,

The coffee brewing

And the windows cracked

And none of that matters

If you don't sit down and

Let it happen.

Apathy

I've spent a lot of time

Learning how to

Shut down.

You've spent a lot of time

Trying to

Wake me up.

We are at odds.

Can't you see that was the problem

In the first place?

Dependable

All I want is what you want

I don't know unless you know

All I hope is what you hope

I'm not home unless you're home

Duality Of Conflict

If the slam of the door

Is the last one I hear

I will be both glad

And crippled by fear

Please. No more.

Please. Come home.

Okay

I can see the subtle

When they see the insurmountable.

It is this:

If only you would

Hold in your heart

Each other

It would all be okay.

We would all be okay.

The whole thing would be

Okay.

Zero

Quite Fit

I dare you to show me a mold

In which you could find me.

I am, by nature, a splinter maker.

Never will I

Quite fit.

Rules Don't Apply

Unlabel me.

Rewrite the book.

Unlearn my name.

Forget the hook.

I'd like to be

My own.

Synergist

To embody only a segment

To classify as a contingent

To qualify as a statistic

Will never be enough.

I want

All of the above and

none of the rest.

64

Count Me Out

When you do this adding

You so like to do,

Leave me

nothing.

I am no number.

No holographic fear.

No quantified success.

I am

being

counted

out.

Unnumbered, Untitled, Unknown

Please let me know

If ever you

Figure me out.

So far

I'm the smudge

On paper

Left by

The eraser.

If you find me,

Let me know.

So far

I am

The smudge of ink

On lines that haven't

Been written yet.

If you find me,

Let me know.

More Works by Teshelle Combs

For Her

Words laced together on behalf of an idea, a place, a world. Poems for the earth, from someone who's lived here all her life. Poems about what it takes to bring life out of death.

For Him

Words assorted for the robust, for the place we love. Poems about the bold and unafraid nature of nature.

For Them

Poems about the turning of the earth, towards and away from one thing to another, and for the idea of "them," from which we also turn away or towards.

For Us

Poems about the delicate fearlessness of the earth and its beginnings and endings. Perhaps it will give these to us if we are up for the learning.

Love Bad

Poems About Love. Not Love Poems.

A book of poems, by me, Teshelle Combs, for the purpose of the investigation of, or rather the accusation of, or rather the commendation of love and all its claims on me. I would say enjoy, but I am trying to be less naive these days.

Love Bad More

Poems About Love. More Or Less.

A continuation of poems about love by me, Teshelle Combs, in honor of the continuous nature of love and how it goes in either direction, regardless of our requests. I hope this book finds you out of control.

Love Bad Best

Poems About Love. Last, Not Best.

The final installment of poems about love, by me, Teshelle Combs, unless there will be more, which is either up to me or up to love, but probably not up to any of us if poetry has anything to do with anything. You are welcome to it, but I would advise a tentative approach.

Breath Like Glass

Poems for love that never lasts.

CORE SERIES

Ava is the kind of girl who knows what's real and what isn't. Nothing in life is fair. Nothing is given freely. Nothing is painless. Every foster kid can attest to those truths, and Ava lives them every day. But when she meets a family of dragon shifters and is chosen to join them as a rider, her very notion of reality is shaken. She doesn't believe she can let her guard down. She doesn't think she can let them in—especially not the reckless, kind-eyed Cale. To say yes to him means he would be hers—her dragon and her companion—for life. But what if Ava has no life left to give?

The System Series

1 + 1 = Dead. That's the only math that adds up when you're in the System. Everywhere Nick turns, he's surrounded by the inevitability of his own demise at the hands of the people who stole his life from him. That is, until those hands deliver the bleeding, feisty, eye-rolling Nessa Parker. Tasked with keeping his new partner alive, Nick must face all the ways he's died and all the things he's forgotten.

Nessa might as well give up. The moment she gets into that car, the moment she lays her hazel eyes on her new partner, her end begins. It doesn't matter that Nick Masters can slip through time by computing mathematical algorithms in his mind. It doesn't matter how dark and handsome and irresistibly cold he is. Nessa has to defeat her own shadows. Together and alone, Nick and Nessa make sense of their senseless fates and fight for the courage to change it all. Even if it means the System wins and they end up...well...dead.

Contact Teshelle Combs

Instagram @TeshelleCombs

Email: teshellecombs@gmail.com

Acknowledgments

Thank you to my Forest, who taught me to look for myself with a bit more effort. Thank you to Nate, my 0, and thank you to those who continue reading my books, without whom my family would most likely starve.